AFFIRMING

Mark D. Chapman

BY WHAT AUTHORITY?

Authority, Ministry and the Catholic Church

Series Editor: Jeffrey John

DARTON · LONGMAN + TODD

First published in 1997 by
Darton, Longman and Todd Ltd
1 Spencer Court
140–142 Wandsworth High Street
London SW18 4JJ

in association with

Affirming Catholicism
St Giles Church
No 4, The Postern
Wood Street, The Barbican
London EC2Y 8BJ

ISBN 0–232–52223–5

Designed by Bet Ayer
Phototypeset by Intype London Ltd
Printed and bound in Great Britain by
Page Bros, Norwich

Affirming Catholicism

Affirming Catholicism is a movement (not an ecclesiastical party) which exists to do two things. We affirm our confidence in our Anglican heritage; and we seek to renew and promote the Catholic tradition within it. Our aim is to explore, explain and share with others both inside and outside the Church a lively, intelligent and inclusive Catholic faith. In the words of our Trust Deed:

> It is the conviction of many that a respect for scholarship and free enquiry has been characteristic of the Church of England and of the Churches of the wider Anglican Communion from earliest times, and is fully consistent with the status of those Churches as part of the Holy Catholic Church. It is desired to establish a charitable educational foundation which will be true both to those characteristics and to the Catholic tradition within Anglicanism ... The object of the foundation shall be the advancement of education in the doctrines and the historical development of the Church of England and the Churches of the wider Anglican Communion, as held by those standing within the Catholic tradition.

Our Publications

These are offered as one means of presenting Anglican Catholic teaching and practice in as clear and accessible a form as possible. Some cover traditional doctrinal and liturgical themes; others attempt to present a well-argued Catholic viewpoint on issues of debate currently facing the Church. There is a list of our series of booklets on page v.

The present series of books is provided, where appropriate, with summaries to sections, and suggested questions which we hope will facilitate personal study or discussion in groups. Other titles in the series are :

Is There an Anglican Way? – Scripture, Church and Reason: New Approaches to an Old Triad Ross Thompson
The Ministry of Deliverance Dominic Walker OGS
Marriage, Divorce and the Church Antony Harvey

To order these publications individually or on subscription, or for further information about the aims and activities of Affirming Catholicism, write to:

The Secretary
Affirming Catholicism
St Giles Church
No 4, The Postern
Wood St
Barbican
London EC2Y 8BJ

Tel 0171–638 1980
Fax 0171–638 1997

Booklets in the Affirming Catholicism series

About the Author

Mark Chapman studied in Oxford and Munich and teaches Doctrine, Church History and Sociology of Religion at Ripon College, Cuddesdon. He is a member of Oxford University Theology Faculty and is also a non-stipendiary priest in the Dorchester-on-Thames team ministry.

He was previously Stephenson Fellow at Sheffield University and has published many articles on the history of theology in England, Germany and the United States, as well as on Anglican ecclesiology.

Contents

BY WHAT
AUTHORITY?

'By What Authority?'

Since the historic debate at Church House on 11 November 1992, and the subsequent ordinations of women to the priesthood, there have been many threats of separation and schism, and some actual departures from the Church of England. Alongside an unexpectedly small number of conversions to the Roman Catholic Church both by clergy and laity, there have also been polemical calls (by, for example, Aidan Nichols) for a 'uniate' Anglican Church in communion with the see of Rome, which would guarantee the survival of the version of Anglican liturgy used by many Anglo-Catholics. An underlying motivation behind this uniate option was outlined by Geoffrey Kirk, the co-ordinator of the opposition 'Cost of Conscience' group, who, at the same time as denying the authority of the Church of England to ordain women to the priesthood, felt no great desire to become a member of what he felt was a predominantly Irish church.[1] It must be said, however, that the vote to ordain women was unexpected, with few opponents appearing to have given much serious consideration

*For notes and references, see p. 45.

about what to do in the event of a positive vote, as the variety of responses testifies.[2]

Such responses come as no great surprise, however, since the debate about the ordination of women brought to a head fundamental issues about the nature of the Church's authority and that of its ministry which have usually (though not always) been festering beneath the surface for well over a hundred years. Indeed, throughout the debates which led up to the vote there was remarkably little discussion of the theology of priesthood,[3] but a great deal of talk about the authority of the Church of England to ordain 'unilaterally'.[4] The same sort of arguments which emerged in the debates over the ordination of women have surfaced at different times previously, particularly in relation to ecumenical dialogue. The proposals for church union in South India, for instance, and later the conversations with the Methodists, were stalled chiefly by arguments about the authority and validity of ministry.

Whether or not women priests are theoretically possible, so the argument goes, the Church of England was wrong in proceeding to ordination, quite simply because it did not have the authority to ordain them. It had no right to interfere unilaterally with the ministry since the priesthood does not belong to the Church of England alone, but is something shared with all those claiming continuity of Catholic order and apostolic succession. Thus, since its authority comes directly through the apostles from Christ himself, the ministry is of the very essence of the Church Catholic, and to change it without consultation and agreement with all other Catholic Churches, would make the Church of England effectively guilty of schism; in short, since we do not have the authority to change the ministry, and since the apostolic ministry is of the very essence of the Church, to ordain women is to unchurch ourselves, and thus to render our sacraments null and void.[5] Cardinal Manning's question, 'By what authority?', which forms the title of this booklet, has thus once again become the central focus for debate in the contemporary Church of England.

There is nothing new in the kind of argument from authority used against the ordination of women: indeed, from at least the beginnings of the Tractarian Movement in 1833, it would probably not be an understatement to say that there has been a fixation on the subject of the authority of the ministry within the Church of England. The context of Manning's question is itself illuminating. It comes from a Journal entry written later in his life on the development of his theology during the 1830s, when he was still an Anglican, and marks perhaps his first serious doubting of his own authority: 'The first question that arose in my mind was, What right have you to be teaching, admonishing, reforming, rebuking others? By what authority do you lift the latch of a poor man's door and enter and sit down and begin to instruct or to correct him? . . . if I was not a messenger sent from God, I was an intruder and impertinent.'[6]

Arguments over the authority of the Church of England became central to the Tractarians as they defended its independent authority as it sought to free itself from an 'apostate' Government's interference in the 1830s. The essential point was this: the Church had its own authority over and against that of Parliament, an authority which stemmed from beyond the national Church and derived ultimately from the apostles themselves. Newman's closest friend, Hurrell Froude (1803–36), who was perhaps the most radical of the Oxford Reformers, put this succinctly in a typical aphorism: 'Let us tell the truth and shame the devil; let us give up a national church and have a real one.'[7]

No Catholic Anglican treatise on authority and ministry can afford to ignore the sheer weight of this Tractarian legacy which places such an extraordinary emphasis on apostolic succession as the source of the independent authority of the Church. In this book I want to tackle the problem of authority head-on since it seems to me to be the most crucial issue facing Catholic Anglicans at the present time. What I will try to show is that the fixation on the authority of the visible Church and its ordained ministry which has dominated so much Anglo-Catholic thinking in the past, while understandable, is nevertheless a fundamental denial of a sense of catholicity which is open to the future. By looking at a few historical episodes in the Anglo-Catholic movement,[8] I will try and draw out the inherent inadequacies and problems of the fixation on the ministry.

The alternative model of authority which I will then go on to outline, which draws primarily from the work of the neglected Mirfield Father, J. N. Figgis, offers a quite different understanding of the Church and the future. Such an understanding, I will claim, while no less Catholic, is far more radical and far more human (even though it will undoubtedly appear to some to be devoid of all real authority).

Summary
The issue of admitting women to ordained ministry in the Anglican Church has caused a crisis in theological understanding of the ministry, particularly among those in the Catholic tradition of the Church. From the beginnings of the Oxford Movement, Anglican Catholics have tended to hold that the Church's authority derives from the 'apostolic succession' – that is, from a supposedly unbroken line of bishops going back to the apostles themselves – and from the threefold ministry of bishops, priests and deacons ordained within that succession.

Anglo-Catholicism and Authority

The Tractarians

If there is one theological theme that characterizes the initial phase of the Catholic revival centred on Oxford in the 1830s, it is that of the authority of the 'apostolic' ministry. Indeed, the very first of the Tracts for the Times (which eventually numbered 90 and gave their name to the movement), written by John Henry Newman and published in September 1833, shortly after John Keble's famous Assize sermon, was entitled *Thoughts on the Ministerial Commission, respectfully addressed to the clergy.* This Tract served to some extent as a manifesto for a rediscovered sense of the authority of the visible Church and particularly of its ministry, which was independent of any secular authority.

'I fear,' wrote Newman, 'we have neglected the last ground on which our authority is built – our apostolical descent.' And he went on to amplify what he meant: 'The Lord Jesus Christ gave his spirit to his apostles; they in turn laid their hands on those who should succeed them; and these again on others; and so the sacred gift has been handed down to our present bishops, who have appointed us as their assistants, and in some sense representatives ... We must necessarily consider *none* to be ordained who have not been *thus* ordained.'[9] And it hardly needed to be said that without a valid ministry, then there was no valid Eucharist, a point emphasized by John Keble in Tract Four, *Adherence to the Apostolical Succession the Safest Course.* Here he claimed that the Church of England was the 'the only Church in this realm which has a right to be quite sure that she has the Lord's Body to give to his people'.[10]

Newman, Keble and their friends were making a stand against what they saw as the Government's legislation for heresy and denial of true religion, which was manifested in such acts as Catholic Emancipation in 1829 and the abolition of certain Irish bishoprics in 1833. And in response to such acts of apparent betrayal by a civil authority which was no longer prepared to defend the Church, they saw it as vital for the Church to find its own authority to defend itself.[11] The 1833 measure was thus regarded by Keble as an outrageous affront on the rights of the Church Catholic, which, he claimed, was a society 'built upon the Apostles and prophets, Jesus Christ himself being the chief cornerstone'. Soon afterwards Newman made his attitudes clear in his great book on the Arian controversy, where he directed his venom as much towards his own period as towards the fourth century: 'Then as now,' he wrote, 'there was the prospect and partly the presence in the Church, of an heretical power enthralling it, exerting a varied influence and a usurped claim in the appointment of her functionaries, and interfering with the management of her internal affairs.'[12]

So if the old ecclesiastical settlement which was based on the Divine Right of Kings (though now exercised by parliamentary sovereignty) had proved itself guilty of apostasy, then it was up to the Church to seek its own independent source of authority: in short, it had to stand on its own two feet. Newman thus wrote to Froude in 1838: 'The King ... has literally betrayed us ... Our first duty is the defence of the Church. We have stood by Monarchy and Authority till they have refused to stand by themselves.'[13]

In an earlier letter of 23 May 1836 to his fellow Tractarian, H. J. Rose, Newman outlined his differences from the much admired Caroline divines of the seventeenth century: 'The single difference between their views and those I seem to follow is this – they had a divine right king – we in matter of fact have not.'[14] Against the heretical acts of the state, the Church had to maintain its own source of sovereignty, as the future Cardinal H. E. Manning preached in Chichester Cathedral in 1835: 'The invisible spiritualities of our apostolical descent, and our ministerial power in the word and sacraments, no prince, no potentate, no apostate nation can sully with a breath of harm.'[15] The radical message of the Tractarians was that the apostolic ministry was the basis of the Church's independent authority, and at the same time part of the very essence of the Church.[16]

Summary

Newman and the Tractarians were originally led to insist on the doctrine of the apostolic succession when Parliament passed certain Acts which they felt interfered with the rights and prerogatives of the Church. It became important to lay down the grounds on which they believed the Church possessed its own authority to teach and govern its own affairs. At the same time they insisted that the apostolic ministry was *essential* for any particular church to have a claim to be part of the true Church, and for its sacraments to be 'valid' sacraments.

The problem of ministry in the late nineteenth century

A similar emphasis on the authority of ministry continued to dominate the ecclesiological thinking of the successors to the Tractarians, probably the most important of whom was Charles Gore (1853–1932), the leader of the third generation of Anglo-Catholics, first principal of Pusey House in Oxford, founder of the Community of the Resurrection and later bishop successively of Worcester, Birmingham and Oxford (and incidentally the originator of the term 'liberal catholicism'). Gore's thinking on ministry and authority emerged partly in response to Edwin Hatch's 1880 Bampton Lectures, *The Organization of the Early Christian Churches.*[17]

Hatch (1835–89), who was one of the foremost Oxford-based historians of the early Church, argued that the Church was 'in no way instituted by Christ to continue his work'. It was instead 'a natural society of believers' and 'came about under the natural laws of providence, and by no special operation of grace'. In relation to the ministry of the Church, Hatch had adopted a view that Church orders were primarily established to fulfil certain functions within the Christian community, and were ultimately a matter of adaptation to circumstances.

In this understanding, Hatch was expanding upon theories developed by J. B. Lightfoot (1828–89), the great Cambridge New Testament Scholar, who eventually became a reforming Bishop of Durham, in his celebrated dissertation on the ministry appended to his commentary on the epistle to the Philippians.[18] Lightfoot's opening words reveal a fundamentally different view of the Church from that of the Tractarians. Instead of stressing the authority of the visible order of the Church, he claimed instead that 'the kingdom of Christ, not being a kingdom of this world . . . has no sacerdotal system. It interposes no sacrificial tribe or class between God and man' (*Philippians*, p.181). Lightfoot held that the invisible kingdom of Christ functioned as the clear ideal, against which any possible understanding of orders in the visible church had to be weighed. Any Church order, he claimed, whether it was presbyterian, congregational or episcopal, was thus a means rather than an end. In short, Church orders were 'aids and expedients' which 'a Christian could not afford to hold lightly or to neglect. But they were no part of the *essence* of God's message to man in the Gospel'. The ministry in the early Church was thus instituted for purely functional (though undoubtedly important) purposes, but 'the priestly functions and privileges of the Christian people [all alike priests in the ideal] are never regarded as transferred or even delegated to these officers' (*Philippians*, p.184).

Even if the threefold ministry (of bishops, priests and deacons) is of a very early origin, according to Lightfoot, it is extremely difficult to find evidence for its being regarded as in any sense sacerdotal (that is, sacred, sacrificing, hierocratic) and thus of the very essence of the Church. Although he recognized that there are hints in the early Fathers of a sacerdotal ministry, especially in Ignatius (active in the latter part of the first century), it was only with St Cyprian in the middle of the third century, with his emphasis on Old Testament notions of priesthood, that there was an 'undisguised' defence of the sacerdotal view of ministry (*Philippians*, p.258).[19] Against the sacerdotal understanding of priesthood which regards the work of the priest as necessary for salvation, Lightfoot claimed instead that the priest was the one who represents God to human beings and human beings to God: the priest's acts are not his own but the acts of the congregation, and are always a means to an end.

The debate on the organization and the ministry of the early Church is even today one of the most hotly disputed in scholarship of Christian origins. Without going into detail, most recent discussions of the New Testament would tend to agree with the sort of conclusion reached by Hatch and Lightfoot and would probably see a number of different 'trajectories' in the organization of ministry in the early Church.[20] However, although there are important distinctions between Hatch and Lightfoot, what I want to emphasize is that both saw ministry to be relative to the community's needs: though some form of ministry was no doubt necessary for the organization of the Church, its precise form was not.

In adopting this position, Hatch and Lightfoot maintained a similar stance to that of many of the early Anglican divines. For instance, in the theological debates in the Elizabethan period, the arguments between the Puritan, Thomas Cartwright (1535–1603) and Archbishop John Whitgift (c.1530–1604) – and later between Walter Travers (c.1548–1635) and Richard Hooker (c.1554–1600) – focused on whether or not a particular Church order was laid down in Scripture and therefore necessary. What is interesting in comparison to the Tractarians is that Whitgift, although a defender of episcopacy, regarded the *form* of the ministry as a matter 'indifferent' and therefore under the proper authority in matters indifferent: the Queen in parliament.[21] Similarly, even those later Divines most admired by the Tractarians – for instance Lancelot Andrewes (1555–1626), the great Bishop of Winchester – refused to see a particular Church order as necessary to salvation. 'If our form be of divine right,' Andrewes wrote, 'it doth not follow from thence that there is no salvation without it, or that a Church cannot consist without it. He is blind who does not see Churches consisting without it ... There may be something absent in the exterior regiment, which is of divine right, and yet salvation to be had.'[22] Similarly John Bramhall (1594–1663), Archbishop of Armagh, was able to concede that the reformed Churches lost 'nothing of the true essence of a Church, though they miss something of their glory and perfection'.[23]

Summary
In contrast to the Tractarians, theologians like Lightfoot and Hatch in the late nineteenth century argued that Jesus did not set up any particular structure for the ministry of his Church, and they underlined the fact that there is no strong authority for the idea of apostolic succession or the threefold ministry in the

New Testament. They also distinguished sharply between the invisible kingdom of God, and the Church, which they saw as essentially a human institution. The seventeenth-century Anglican divines also, for the most part, did not view the episcopal system as laid down in Scripture, and did not deny that salvation could be found outside it.

Bishop Gore's response

Bishop Gore's response to the traditional Anglican position maintained by Hatch and Lightfoot was characterized by a return to the Tractarian emphasis which placed great weight on the authority of the visible Church. Thus in his first lengthy book, *The Church and the Ministry* of 1888, he asserts that the means cannot be separated from the ends: the visible Church is thus equated with the Kingdom of God: 'Christ has instituted a Kingdom of means, a visible channel for His covenanted gifts of grace'.[24] Consequently, unlike Lightfoot, Gore is not content to leave the ordering of ministry to the devising of human beings, but sees it as somehow necessarily constituted by Christ's authority. Thus he says: 'Christianity is as much the establishment of a visible system of means for realising the end of human life, as it is the divine announcement of what that end is' (*The Church and the Ministry*, p.355). Gore thus spends a great deal of time trying to prove that Christ founded a visible Church and that this had from the outset a necessary organizational structure. Basing his argument on what would now be considered the rather dubious attribution of the Pastoral epistles to Paul, Gore wrote: 'the record of history renders it practically indisputable that Jesus Christ founded a visible society or Church, to be the organ of his spirit in the world, the depository of his truth, the covenanted sphere of his redemptive grace and discipline' (*The Church and the Ministry*, p.337). The succession of orders, most importantly in the episcopate, thus became the channel of authority from Christ himself (*The Church and the Ministry*, p.343). Consequently, all Church union had to be based on the principle of apostolic succession.

Gore later made a similar point succinctly in a speech delivered at an ecumenical conference on the priesthood held in 1899: 'In my opinion the very essence of Christianity is the conception that Christ is realized in the visible body of the Church, and everything that weakens that conception is to be deprecated. It is in and through corporate fellowship that we realize all that is possible for us as individuals.'[25] According to Gore, Christ founded a visible and hierarchical society, and the contemporary Church was a successor to that society; and furthermore, he argued, if Christ founded no such society, then the whole basis of our salvation would be null and void. Similarly, in a 1909 discussion of ministry, Gore once again included the apostolic ministry within the very essence of the Church:

> [All] Christians recognize that there are fundamental elements in the Church which are not within the Church's legislative power: which come out of a religion anterior to, and higher than its own historical life: which were given it or imposed upon it by the authority of Christ its founder. Such elements are the sacraments of baptism and the Eucharist, and the ordinance of monogamy, and the authority of the Old Testament Scriptures: among these elements – I contend – is the ministry, if not in form, yet in principle and authority.[26]

As this last sentence makes clear, the defence of ministry, for Gore, is a defence of the Church's unique source of authority: without the apostolic ministry the Church simply loses its authority. In an earlier discussion of *Roman Catholic Claims*, Gore remarked in a similar vein: 'Every Church which claims her following in the catholic fraternity must be prepared not only to show that she is not wilfully schismatical but also, and before that, to meet two legitimate challenges – to vindicate her orthodoxy and to vindicate her order, that is, her claim to be within the historical succession of the Church's life.'[27] No Church is catholic, according to Gore, which does not have these tests.

The obvious implication of Gore's thought is that all those who do not have this form of ministry are thereby unchurched, since they have 'violated a fundamental principle of the Church's life' and do not possess the 'security of the covenant'.[28] Thus, by strictly following the logic of the Tractarian tradition, it becomes clear that for Gore, the ministry (admittedly together with orthodoxy) makes the Church, and also that its authority depends not chiefly on what it does or says, but rather on its standing in continuity with its predecessors. Indeed, what becomes vital for any Church to be called Catholic is that its orders can be vindicated. In turn, the natural extension of this understanding of ministerial authority is to make salvation dependent on the sacramental system of the visible Church exercised by a validly ordained ministry.

R. C. Moberly, Gore and the clamour for authority

A not dissimilar form of argument for the indispensability of visible order was offered by the Oxford Professor of Pastoral Theology, R. C. Moberly (1845–1903) in his highly influential book *Ministerial Priesthood*, first published in 1897,[29] and somewhat dominated by the debate on 'validity' which followed on from the declaration of the nullity of Anglican orders by Leo XIII in the Bull *Apostolicae Curae* of 1896.[30] Although Moberly anticipated many of the ideas which would later become commonplace, especially the linking of sacerdotal and ministerial aspects of priesthood,[31] he also vigorously maintained the doctrine of apostolic succession as the chief basis of ministerial authority: 'The Church disciplined, purified, perfected, – shall be found to be the kingdom; the kingdom of heaven is already, in the Church, among men. Scripture, which knows so well both the Church and the Kingdom, knows nothing of any antithesis between them' (*Ministerial Priesthood*, p.37). The gap between the Church and the Kingdom of God which had been maintained by Lightfoot had thus been bridged by Moberly:

> The visible Body is the spiritual Church – is so really . . . In external truth, the most primary, the most obvious to the eye, the Church is a human society, with experience chequered like the experience of human societies; in its inner reality, it is the presence and the working, here and now, of the leaven of the spirit; it does not represent

– but it *is* – the Kingdom of God upon earth. (*Ministerial Priesthood*, p.40)

By applying some rather tortuous logic Moberly is led to assert that the contingent facts of history and the spiritual truths of the Kingdom can become one in a new synthesis (*Ministerial Priesthood*, p.58).

In reading these late Victorian defences of the necessity of the apostolic ministry of the Church, it becomes clear that there was a striving after some kind of certain authority which, while not necessarily infallible (in that it was not beyond all possible criticism), nevertheless had absolute sovereignty over all those who chose to submit. Charles Gore opens himself up to this charge since he eventually admitted (in *Orders and Unity*) that he had failed to prove that the most primitive form of church government resembled the contemporary threefold ministry and was founded directly by Christ. Indeed, he ultimately recognized that the New Testament could not yield any conclusive evidence:

> It must be admitted that if the documents of the New Testament stood alone – if Christianity had vanished from the world and these documents had been disinterred and constituted our sole evidence of the nature of ancient religion – we should feel that various tendencies towards different kinds of organization were at work in the Christian Church, that the picture presented was confused, and that no decisive conclusion as to the form of the Christian ministry could be reached. But in fact the documents of the NT are only some of the documents which belong to a great historical movement. And the tendency of the whole movement – the disentangling of

tendencies and the emergence of dominant principles – guides us in attributing more or less importance to this or that phenomenon. The earliest history must be interpreted in the light of what emerged from it as the regular and universally accepted order. (*Orders and Unity*, p.83)

There is an inherent inconsistency here: Gore cannot see the threefold ministry as definitively revealed in Scripture, yet he believes it to be necessary. He therefore commits a significant act of submission: the ministry *must* have evolved by what he calls in *The Church and the Ministry* a 'common instinct'; thus he claimed that 'everywhere there was a development which made unerringly for the same goal. This seems to speak of a divine institution almost as plainly as if our Lord had in so many words prescribed this form of church government' (p.303). The fact of a universal episcopacy in the early Church simply *proves* that in some sense it must have been initiated by Christ.

Gore claimed that he had adopted what he called the 'liberal' method, which saw Scripture as the 'final testing ground of the dogmatic claims of the Church ... The scriptural test, frequently re-iterated in our formularies, is the safeguard of liberty against the constant tendency to exaggerate ecclesiastical authority and to accumulate dogma. It is this appeal ... which qualifies the Catholicism of the Church of England as Scriptural or liberal.'[32] However, what was ultimately more important for Gore than this method was the need for a 'certain' authority to which human beings could submit; true authority, he argued, was 'parental': 'it invigorates and encourages, even while it restrains and guides the growth of our individuality' (*Roman Catholic Claims*, p.51).

This emphasis on a voluntary submission to the visible authority of the Church is at the same time entry into its universal fellowship, and even the means by which the disintegrating and alienating effects of modern life are overcome. Thus, although Gore may have called himself a liberal, it seems that it is submission to a visible authority, rather than rational and critical appraisal of that authority, which rests at the heart of his theological system. Thus he wrote in *Roman Catholic Claims*:

> I must protest that the authority of the Church is, as we Anglicans understand it, a most real guidance of our spirit and intellect to which, by God's mercy, we love to submit ourselves. Submission to that authority is the merging of our mere individualism in the whole historic life of the great Christian brotherhood; it is making ourselves at one with the one religion in its most permanent and least merely local form. It is surrendering our individuality only to empty it of its narrowness. One with the Christianity of history, the Christianity of creeds and councils, we enter into the heritage of her dogmas and of something as great as her greatest dogmas, the whole joy of her sacraments, the security of her ministry, the communion of her saints, the fellowship of her spirit. We can read her great fathers and find ourselves one with them in all matters of faith over the lapse of ages. The hearts of the fathers are seen to be turned towards their children. We believe in the Holy Catholic Church. (pp.51f.)

The dangers and the authoritarian character of such claims were well recognized by the Congregationalist, A. M. Fairbairn (1838–1912), Principal of Mansfield College, Oxford. The ministry was no longer a means to an end but had become the 'pillar and ground of truth' and was consequently beyond all criticism.[33]

For the Tractarians and later for Bishop Gore it is thus quite clear that the quest for authority was behind their elevation of the apostolic ministry into the very essence of the Church, a position which has been maintained by many others since. Thus, in his editorial introduction to an influential collection of essays entitled *The Apostolic Ministry*, Kenneth Kirk (1886–1954), Bishop of Oxford, wrote: 'It is only as she can claim that her ministry derives from the Lord himself in the days of his flesh, and is given her for leadership, for path-finding and for spiritual replenishment, that she can pursue her victorious yet dreadful pilgrimage undaunted.'[34]

Such an understanding of authority was to expand into the vacuum left by the final collapse of the fiction of the late medieval theory of imperial sovereignty which Henry VIII had attempted to impose on the Church of England. This collapse was symbolized for the Tractarians by Catholic Emancipation and the abolition of the Irish Bishops. Harold Laski could thus characterize Tractarianism as 'essentially the plea of the corporate body which is distinct from the State to a separate and free existence'.[35] Indeed, it comes as no great surprise to learn that many of the successors to the Tractarians in the Anglo-Catholic movement, including Gore himself, moved towards disestablishment: 'From the point of view alike of Church and State ... a "free church" in a "free state" is in some real sense the only possible political ideal, at least for a democratically governed country like England.'[36]

However, in discussing this clamour for authority, while it is easy to be sympathetic towards the Tractarian Fathers and their successors who sought to restore to the Church its independence, it is nevertheless far more difficult to see their emphasis on submission to what amounts to ministerial authority as in any real sense a viable alternative to the breakdown of unified model of Church and society under the Divinely appointed sovereign which had guided the original Anglican settlement. Indeed, the rediscovery of the apostolic authority might more cynically be viewed as perhaps little more than an attempt to bolster clerical power. It can hardly be accidental that accompanying the revival of ministerial authority in the nineteenth century there were major changes in the style of Anglican architecture and worship, most of which served to emphasize the distinction between clergy and laity as well as increasing the focus on the sacerdotal power of the priest. This point was noted by the pioneer of the Gothic revival, the Roman Catholic convert, A. W. Pugin, in 1843: 'It is most delightful to see the feeling reviving in the Anglican Church for the sanctity and depths of chancels; and as a preliminary step to better things, it should receive all possible encouragement, but those who think merely to build chancels, without reviving the ancient faith, will be miserably deceived in their expectations.'[37]

In the remainder of this book I want to outline an alternative model of ecclesial authority which does not succumb to the enticements of submission to a supernatural doctrine of the divine origins and legitimation of the Church's ministry, but which instead redirects the focus of authority towards the future. I also want to maintain that this alternative model of authority is no less Catholic, but at the same time that it is a great deal more humble.

Summary
Gore and Moberly restated the Tractarian view which emphasized the authority of the visible Church, and virtually identified it with the Kingdom of God. They saw possession of the apostolic ministry as the main evidence of the Church's authority and claim to be 'catholic', and so insisted that maintaining it was essential in any move towards Church union. In the absence of strong New Testament evidence, and believing that a visible authority must have been willed by God, Gore argued that the evolution of the threefold apostolic ministry in the second century made it *practically speaking* an institution of Christ himself.

Another Model of Catholic Authority: the Vision of J. N. Figgis

What I think is most at fault in the theology of Bishop Gore and of the Tractarians is their over-emphasis on the authority of the visible Church, which is always conceived as something existing somehow independently of and external to the contemporary Christian. Their emphasis seems to have rested on the idea that the Christian is *connected* to the body of Christ in so far as he or she submitted to the Church which derived its authority from Christ. The sense in which the contemporary Christian was actually part of the eternal body of Christ and *shared* in the authority of that body in communion with all other Christians, past, present, and future, seems to have been lacking in the fixation on visibility, apostolicity and ministry.

There is thus little notion in the Tractarians and Gore of the inter-relationship of all authority: it is as though the contemporary Christian did not share in the authority of the Church, but had instead to submit to something which was channelled by some direct pipeline from the generation of the apostles (and which would now be considered to have extremely leaky plumbing). On this understanding, all authority derived ultimately from the past: the role of the present day Christian as well as of future generations was to submit to a Church orientated towards a fixed tradition which had little scope for any reshaping in the light of any future goal. In distinction to this model, it seems to me to be possible to reconceive authority as orientated towards the future but nevertheless shaped by past and present. This points the Catholic vision away from a concentration on the past towards an authoritative yet ultimately unknowable future. Since it always lies beyond human grasp, the authority of this future can never be absolute or authoritarian but nevertheless it has some kind of authority since it is in this future that God will reign in his glory.

Before looking at a notion of authority located primarily in the future, I want to discuss a model of authority which takes seriously the inter-relationship between all Christians past, present and future as they share in the authority of the Church.

I have developed this from the writings of John Neville Figgis (1866–1919) and will offer a number of short extracts from three of his books. Figgis was the son of a Brighton minister of the Countess of Huntingdon's Connexion and educated at St Catharine's College, Cambridge, where he came under the influence of the historian and future Bishop of London, Mandell Creighton, as well as the political and legal theorist, F. W. Maitland. After ordination, he lectured at St Catharine's from 1896–1902. After experiencing severe health problems he became Rector of Marnhull in Dorset from 1902 to 1907, and in 1907 was received into the Community of the

Resurrection after seeing a play by Bernard Shaw. For the rest of his life he alternated in a 'regular pendulum motion between Mirfield fasts and Cambridge feasts'. He gave the Cambridge Hulsean lectures in 1908 and lectured on two occasions in the USA, during 1913 and 1915. In January 1918, while travelling to the USA for another lecture tour, his ship was torpedoed and shipwrecked off the coast of Antrim, where his manuscript on Bossuet was lost. He never recovered from the trauma and spent his last days in a mental hospital in Virginia Water.[38]

Perhaps Figgis' most important contribution to the theology of authority rests in his recognition of the ultimately limited character of any authority which could be exercised by a Church in a modern pluralist society, since it depended no longer on the status or claims of a particular institution or person, but on the individual's decision to accept something or somebody as authoritative. Thus even though the authority of the Church might be accepted as infallible, it was only so in relation to the individual's conscience. And that meant, where conscience was offended, the individual could always remove obedience and find another Church, or at least try to create another one within an existing Church.

Indeed, whatever the theory, this has been the form of authority actually demonstrated by many Anglo-Catholics in practice. Thus Principal Fairbairn remarked: the clergy who plead most 'for an apostolic episcopate as the condition for Catholic Unity, defer least to the episcopal voice'.[39] Or as Frank Weston, the great Bishop of Zanzibar, put it during the heady days of Anglo-Catholic triumphalism in the 1920s: 'I am not asking for obedience to a bishop. I ask for obedience to the bishops in so far as they themselves obey the Catholic Church.'[40] Even Gore is reported as saying: 'As for Bishops, they are hopeless; I have done with them.'[41]

However, the form of authority which Figgis had in mind was not merely that of obedience in the light of a good conscience. He went further and looked at a concept of authority which was *dependent* upon the active participation of all members, and which was nothing apart from this. He likens this form of authority to that found in the rowing eight, where each member of the crew is as vital as all the others and each contributes his or her own part, but only in relation to the crew as a unit. The unit and the individuals are thus both vitally interrelated to one another. Authority is thus at once external to the individual and yet also immanent within the individual. The individual, like the oarsman, is a part of the greater whole, and yet the greater whole would be nothing without the participating individuals. When applied to the Church, this meant if nobody joined and participated in the Church it would not exist so could have no authority. Thus Figgis wrote:

> Authority in religion is the spirit of that vast super-individual life of the whole society, which surrounds its living members like an atmosphere, to which all without exception contribute some element, and which sometimes, though rarely, becomes crystallized in definite

commands and creeds. Authority is the expression of the sociality of man ... It arises from the fact that individuals, bound together in community for permanent ends, are changed by their union; that the life of the community and its members is spiritual and interpenetrating. (*The Fellowship of the Mystery*, pp.188f)

The external and the internal were thus vitally and necessarily related to one another. Thus, where the emphasis of the Tractarians as well as of the resurgent ultramontane Roman Catholic Church had been to emphasize the authority of the external and visible Church, Figgis maintained the interconnection between the internal and the external. Quite simply, the one could not exist without the other. This meant that for the Church there had to be a continual dialogue and sharing between all members in a living form of authority:

What we most need to realize is that authority in the Church of God is the expression of the life of the whole Christian community, and no single member but plays his part. Of all dangers which beset the statement of the idea of authority, none at this moment is so serious as that which views it purely as external command. The moment that notion is accepted, we are far on the way to the notion that the duty of the majority is merely passive. (*Fellowship*, p.193)

Figgis' whole system is based upon the interpenetration of the group and the individual, and the need for the individual continually to consent to the group. This process of consent is that of weighing up one's membership (albeit cautiously and deferentially), but ultimately having to decide for oneself on the legitimacy of the coercive authority of the group. Support could always be withdrawn:

> If the individual only comes to himself as part of a society, his conscience is always partially social. Why should not the society which has made him what he is assert an authority in the last resort coercive against him? It may, and I think ought, to be said that the authority of society is no more than a very strong presumption; in the last resort the individual must decide, and persecution denies this. (*Churches in the Modern State*, pp.116f)

Figgis' understanding of authority is thus based on his theory of personality as something which can never reside solely in the individual but is something which brings the individual into the broader historical and social sphere:

> the individual cannot come to himself except in a society. That is the ever-repeated lesson of the family, the school, the college, and of all the thousand and one developments of the associative principle in life. (*Fellowship*, p.50)

It was impossible to see individuals in isolation; indeed the very primary institutions of family, school and economics ensured there was a degree of socialisation (even when this was not recognized):

> For in truth the notion of isolated individuality is the shadow of a dream, and would never have come into being but for the vast social structure which allows a few individuals to make play, as though they were independent, when their whole economic position of freedom is

symbolic of a long history and complex social organization. In the real world, the isolated individual does not
exist; he begins always as a member of something,
and ... his personality can develop only in society ...
Membership in a social union means a direction of personality, which interpenetrates it. (*CMS*, p.88)

Social institutions thus form the very basis of individuality. In turn there is the need for the proper balance
between the individual and the group, or in the
Church, between the particular and Catholic.

Authority was thus not about passive obedience but
meant active participation in an authority intimately
bound up with the decision to join the Church in the
first place: yet such a decision was not about submit-
ting to a dead past, but rather required a constant
process of re-commitment and reweighing, which,
Figgis claimed, formed the basis of the real fellowship
of the Church. Indeed, it was a positive benefit that
the Church no longer had the coercive power to
ensure blind obedience. The advantage of toleration,
according to Figgis, 'is that it acts automatically on
the purity of religious bodies and the reality of their
faith; and, where complete, it produces a temper
which, annealed in the fires of constant criticism, is
analogous to that produced by persecution in the
earlier days of the Church' (*CMS*, p.119).

Even more crucial in Figgis's understanding of
authority was his insistence that the authority of the
universal Church was necessary not in itself but only
when it was required to settle disputes, and it was
always relative to particular problems. This meant that

the local and particular church was always prior to the universal: indeed the universal Church was very much a body which depended for its authority on the groups which comprised it, and who yielded to it a realm for adjudication in disputes. Indeed, its authority was no more than this, which inevitably meant that the authority of the groups of groups, the Church Catholic, was highly fluid and disorganized. Ultimately, then, all authority came not from above, but from below (cf. *CMS*, pp.146ff.). Thus Figgis claimed:

> I do not believe that there is in the universe an authority rigidly absolute, in the sense of an ultramontane legalist; God himself does not command us, independent of reason and conscience. The truth rather sees the spirit of Christ, the authority in the Christian body as a whole, and does not concentrate it in a centre, not even in a general council. In every organic part of it there is the Church. (*Fellowship*, p.202)

The Church existed because it comprised those who had voluntarily chosen to accept its authority, but it was not effectively sovereign over them, since they were open to remove their allegiance and had constantly to reaffirm commitment. This understanding of authority implies a view of tradition, not as something stuck in the past, either in the sacred book of the Protestant Churches, or indeed the councils of the first four Christian centuries, but rather as something which had to live in each new period. 'Too often,' wrote Figgis, 'has Christianity become identified with mere tradition or outward respectability. Too often it is treated, not as a living spirit, but as a dead deposit' (*Fellowship*, p.83). Indeed, it was all too easy for something which should be liberating to become oppressive:

> While the ceremonious and critical pronouncements of the Church organs at momentous epochs are in all ages to be received with deference, and indeed may come to us with a weight which is only not overwhelming, I can see no ground for supposing that they are infallible in such a way as to deny the living power of the Church in the present and the future, or to deliver us bound to the 'dead hand'. It is this enslavement of the present to the past which is feared by many just now; nor are their fears altogether without ground – so mistaken is the conception of the authority entertained by many, and the confusion of the real weight to be attached to tradition with a certainty which would only too literally be 'dead'. (*Fellowship*, p.197)

Authority consequently rested in the living body of Christ and could neither be isolated in a particular moment, nor in a particular institution, however magisterial. It was thus quite simply impossible to step outside of our own age into the past (even though the past will always shape our own age): 'Each age does not merely carry on; it transcends all ages before it' (*Fellowship*, p.60). Figgis identifies this sense of transcendence with catholicity, which is something constantly moving us beyond our inherent desire to rest content with our own partial expressions of Christianity into a reweighing and resifting for the sake of the future. Ultimately no one part of the Church, no one source of authority, can ever claim itself to be *the* Catholic Church. Figgis thus writes:

> If the Church be what we claim that she is, Catholic, the true and universal home of the spirit of man, we must beware of any view of her which would crystallize her life at any moment, either of the past or the present; and we must see to it that our boast is justified that in her the spiritual treasures are richer, freer, and more varied than in any other society. (*Fellowship*, p.69)

All the resources of the past, present and, most crucially, future thus had to be embraced in the vision of catholicity which was not to be an imprisonment in a dubious submissive form of authority.

The redefinition of the nature of authority was thus at the same time a redefinition of catholicity:

> One can find Churches preening themselves on their Catholic heritage, while in reality they have nothing to show but an arid legalism, unless it be a yet more futile antiquarianism. We can use the Catholic vision to our profit only as we interpret it to mean the power of a living Church to free all the elements that come down to it, to reinterpret and transcend the past; all other use of them will land us in disaster. (p.73)

Ultimately, then, what was important was loyalty to this sense of wholeness, a wholeness that could never be reduced to any simple or single expression, on account of a loyalty to 'the splendour of [the Church's] future glory; – that is the root of the matter'. Figgis goes on to ask: 'When a man feels that he has that, who are we that we should lightly charge him with dishonour, merely because he applies in one place methods of exegesis which each of us applies elsewhere?' (*Fellowship*, pp.269f). The Church Catholic was thus founded upon a vision of unity which embraced past, present and future, and thus surpassed and transcended any expression which had hitherto been achieved. This glorious future served to limit all expressions of absoluteness and any attempt to identify the fullness of God's truth with something given.

Figgis' vision of a decentralized and organic Church is practical and pragmatic, and yet at the same time always in flux as new insights and a changing perspective engendered new experiments and new ideas. This was 'the direct opposite' of the ultramontane theory where all authority is gathered at the centre. Instead '[the] authority of the Church is not an abstract doctrine deduced from the notion of unity; but is a synthesis of all the living parts of the Church. True, a connection exists between them, or one could not talk of the Catholic Church'. However, he goes on: '[any] universal constitution to which we might approach, would be ultimately of the federalist type' (*CMS*, p.166). For Figgis there could be no infallible sovereign authority of any kind, and neither could the usages of one little bit of Christendom (whether Rome or Canterbury) be necessarily and universally right. Indeed, he writes:

> A mere provincial Anglicanism is no religion wherewith to convert the world, pleasing though it be to the historical sentimentalist dwelling in the Caroline climate, or expressive of the nice propensities of ancient country towns. (*Fellowship*, p.68)

In drawing this discussion of Figgis' contribution to

the understanding of authority to a close I hope that I have shown that there is a viable Catholic alternative to the concept of authority maintained by the Tractarians and by Bishop Charles Gore. His most important point, I think, was his realization that authority did not depend upon a submission to some ultimately arbitrary isolation of one little piece of Christian history nor to a particular magisterial authority, but rather authority depended upon the free choice of individuals in favour of something they had weighed and submitted to scrutiny for the sake of continuing transformation: the final authority rested ultimately in the future.

Authority for the Future

Figgis may perhaps be a rather unknown figure on which to base a theory of shared Catholic authority orientated to the future,[42] but there are many others who have redirected the basis for unity and authority away from the past into an unknown and open future which limits all claims of the past. For Anglican Catholics the most important thinker in this connection is probably Michael Ramsey, whose *The Gospel and the Catholic Church* over and over again emphasizes a future which limits any partial claim of the present or the past. Briefly stated, what was important about the Church for Ramsey was that it should bear witness, not to the perfection of those who share in it,

> but to the Gospel of God by which alone, in which alone, in one universal family, mankind can be made perfect. It is not something Roman or Greek or Anglican; rather does it declare to men their utter dependence upon Christ by setting forth the universal Church in which all that is Anglican or Roman or Greek or partial or local in any way must share in an agonizing death to its pride.[43]

The constant subjection of any authority to the annihilating image of the cross served to deliver the

Christian 'from partial rationalisms' into an 'orthodoxy which no individual and no group can possess.
As he receives the Catholic sacrament and recites the
Catholic creed, the Christian is learning that no single
movement nor partial experience within Christendom
can claim his final obedience, and that a local
church can claim his loyalty only by leading him
beyond itself to the universal family which it represents. Hence the Catholic order is not a hierarchical
tyranny, but the means of deliverance into the Gospel
of God and the timeless Church' (*Gospel and the
Catholic Church*, p.135). For Ramsey, then, there is
an ultimate critical point to which everything in the
Church is subjected. And it serves to put to death all
reliance on human achievement, human meaning and
human authority. (It ought to be mentioned, however,
that at times Ramsey somewhat overstates the importance of episcopacy: it is occasionally, although
inconsistently, almost elevated to a level higher than
the Gospel, and becomes of the *esse* of the Church.)[44]

What Figgis, Ramsey, and many others,[45] make clear
is that authority in the Church is neither a question
of institutional validity nor of sovereignty, but a move
away from human authority towards an authority
which relativizes and transcends any human claims.
Indeed human authority, including the visible and
institutional authority of the Church Catholic is
characterized by provisionality or partiality and subjected to criticism in the light of a future where God's
reign will be fully manifest. This emphasis on provisionality might serve to show that being a Catholic
is about sharing in the past, present and future; and

such sharing has something to do with learning to live *without* human authority in the hope that divine authority will emerge as the visible body of Christ more closely resembles its risen, ascended yet ultimately unknowable Lord. In short, authority will always be provisional until such time as that unknown Lord is revealed in his glory.

But as long as that Lord remains unknown, as Catholics we are charged to live towards the future and subject all our authorities to the one who refused authority and power. And that is the act of submission to a divine authority which is yet to be revealed, and as such can only ever lead to humility and provisionality. But that, I think, is what visible Catholic truth is like: a fallible truth proclaimed by fallible human beings who long for a Kingdom which is yet to come. The clamour for authority and finality may be explicable, especially in a world where the old certainties are collapsing, but whatever authority we might claim, and whatever infallibility we might accept can only ever be *our* infallibility and *our* authority.

That means that all authority is partial, limited and open to the future: our Catholic vision transcends all authority and that ultimately is where the tradition of Christ crucified and risen points. The Catholic Church, Michael Ramsey reminds us, is forced to be a Church constantly under judgement, constantly open to reformation; one which subjects its pride to the humiliation of the cross. For, says Ramsey, 'these are Catholicism's own themes, and out of them it was born. But they are themes learnt and relearnt in humiliation, and Catholicism always stands before the Church door at Wittenberg to read the truth by which she is created and by which she is to be judged' (*Gospel and the Catholic Church*, p.180).

Summary
Figgis saw the authority of the Church as deriving not simply from an unchanging, past tradition mediated through the hierarchy of bishops, priests and deacons. For him it was a shared, consensual authority, to which all Christians, past, present and future, in different ways contribute. That authority may be focused in the Church's ordained ministers and articulated by them; but it does not wholly derive from them, nor can it be exercised in isolation from the whole body of the faithful. Rather, it is realized through continual dialogue and sharing between all the Church's members in active participation, not passive obedience. This applies not only to the relations between individuals and the Church, but to the relations between individual churches and the universal Church. Tradition itself is not a dead deposit handed on unchanged, but a living, developing thing which arises from this continuing exchange within the whole body. For Ramsey too (though he set a very high value on episcopacy), the institutional authority of the Church cannot be crystallized into an infallible system: it is always provisional, open to the future, and constantly subject to judgement and reformation.

Questions

'*By what Authority?*'
1. Why have many Catholic Anglicans in particular been distressed by the ordination of women deacons, priests and bishops?

2. How would you explain the idea of apostolic succession? Why was it so crucial to the Tractarians?

3. What other signs of authority are present in the Anglican Church? How do these relate to the ordained ministry?

Anglo-Catholicism and Authority
The Tractarians
1. Newman wrote on the subject of the necessity of ordination by a bishop in the apostolic succession, 'We must necessarily consider *none* to be ordained who have not been *thus* ordained'. If this were true, what would it mean in practice?

2. How useful is the idea of 'validity' as applied to sacraments such as ordination and the Eucharist?

3. Why did Newman think that the situation of the Church of England in 1833 was similar to that of

the Catholic Church in the time of the Arian controversy?

4. What do you feel about the powers which Parliament still has over the life of the Church of England today? Should the Church be disestablished?

The problem of ministry in the late nineteenth century
1. What evidence is there in the New Testament of Jesus laying down any order of ministry in the Church?

2. How do you think the 'kingdom of God' or the 'kingdom of Christ' in the Gospels relates to the visible Church?

3. Do you think all forms of ministry in the Church are equally valid? What are the practical arguments for and against an episcopal system?

4. What did Lightfoot and Hatch mean by attacking a 'sacerdotal', 'sacrificing' or 'hierocratic' understanding of the ministry? Is there a good sense in which the priesthood *ought* to be any of these things?

5. As described by this author, what is the difference between the view of Lightfoot and Hatch about the importance of episcopal ministry, and the view of Lancelot Andrewes and John Bramhall? Which is closer to yours?

R. C. Moberly, Gore, and the clamour for authority
1. What patterns of ministry appear in St Paul's letters? Why was it important for Gore to believe that the Pastoral letters were written by Paul?

2. How did Gore try to get round the fact that the New Testament does not give a clear picture of ordained ministry in the early Church? Is there any force in his argument?

3. What was the danger that Fairburn detected in Gore's ideas?

4. Is it fair to describe the theories of Gore, Moberly and the Tractarians as an attempt to bolster clerical power? Would it be a fair charge to lay against Catholic traditionalists today?

5. What connection does the author see between the development of Tractarian ideas about ministerial authority and contemporary developments in church architecture? Is there a similar link between attitudes to authority and developments in church architecture today?

Authority for the future
1. What does this author see as the main flaw in the view of authority put forward by Gore and the Tractarians? Do you agree with him?

2. Fairburn noted the irony that Anglo-Catholics who most vigorously defended the authority of bishops in theory were often those who most flouted it in practice. Has anything changed?

3. How does Figgis' vision of a shared authority focused in the ordained ministry match up to the situation in the Anglican Church today?

4. How might Figgis' idea of authority affect one's

approach to current issues such as the ordination of women or the acceptability of same-sex relationships?

5. Figgis was determined that Catholicism should not mean an 'arid legalism' or 'antiquarianism'. What should it mean?

6. What did Ramsey mean by Catholicism 'standing by the Church door at Wittenberg to read the truth by which she is created and by which she is to be judged'? How do you see the Church standing under judgement today?

Notes and References

1. See *The Guardian*, 9 April 1993.

2. On this, see, for example, Roger Greenacre, *'Epistola ad Romanos*: an open letter to some Roman Catholic friends' in *The Month*, March 1993, pp.88–96.

3. I have looked at the theology of priesthood elsewhere. See my 'Preparing for judgement: a theology for ministry' in *Modern Believing* New Series XXXVII, No.1, January 1996, pp.10–16.

4. These arguments have been excellently discussed by Henry Chadwick in what is, however, a rather inconclusive essay: 'Making and remaking in the ministry of the Church' in *The Making and Remaking of Christian Doctrine*, edited by Sarah Coakley and David Pailin (Oxford, Clarendon Press, 1993), pp.13–27.

5. I have argued elsewhere for the inherent catholicity of provincial autonomy. See 'Catholicity, unity and provincial autonomy: on making decisions unilaterally', in *Anglican Theological Review*, Vol.76, No.3, Summer 1994, pp.313–28.

6. Cited in E. S. Purcell, *Life of Manning* (London, Macmillan, 1895), Vol.I, p.112.

7. Hurrell Froude, *Remains of the Late Richard Hurrell Froude, MA* (London and Derby, 1838–9), 4 Vols., Vol.III, p.274.

8. Almost any period in Anglican history could be used to illustrate the problem of authority. I have looked at some issues of authority in the Laudian period in 'Cyprianus Anglicus: St Cyprian

and the future of Anglicanism' in *The Future of Anglicanism* (Leominster, Gracewing, 1996).

9. *Thoughts on the Ministerial Commission, respectfully addressed to the clergy* (London, Rivington, 1833), passim.

10. Tract Four, *Adherence to the Apostolical Succession the Safest Course* (London, Rivington, 1833), p.4.

11. On the intricate political background to the Tractarian Movement, see Peter Nockles, *The Oxford Movement in Context* (Cambridge, Cambridge University Press, 1994), esp. pp.67ff. Nockles regards the real beginnings of the Oxford Movement in Oxford University's repudiation of Peel over his support of Catholic Emancipation in 1829 (p.69).

12. *The Arians of the Fourth Century* (London, Pickering, 1883), p.406.

13. Newman to Froude, 8 Sept. 1838 in *The Letters and Diaries of John Henry Newman* (Oxford, Oxford University Press, 1978–84), Vol.IV, p.33.

14. *Letters and Diaries*, Vol.V, p.304.

15. H. E. Manning, *The English Church: its Succession and Witness for Christ*, p.21. Cited in David Newsome, *The Parting of Friends* (London, John Murray, 1966), p.204.

16. See esp. Nockles, *The Oxford Movement*, p.81.

17. Published in London by Longmans, Green and Co, 1881. On this debate see Stephen Mayor, 'Discussion of the ministry in late nineteenth-century Anglicanism' in *The Church Quarterly*, Vol.2 (1969), pp.54–62; and idem, 'The Anglo-Catholic understanding of the ministry: some Protestant comments' in *The Church Quarterly*, Vol.2 (1969), pp.152–9.

18. 1865; refs to 6th ed. (London, Macmillan, 1881).

19. This whole subject is covered polemically by E. Schillebeeckx in *Ministry* (London, SCM, 1981), pp.48ff. See also Maurice Wiles,

'The theological legacy of St Cyprian' in *Journal of Ecclesiastical History*, Vol.14 (1963), pp.139–49.

20. See, for example, J. M. Robinson and H. Koester, *Trajectories Through Early Christianity* (Philadelphia, Fortress Press, 1971), especially pp.13–16.

21. On this, see the *Parker Society* edition of the works of John Whitgift, Vol.I, p.179 and Vol.II, p.97.

22. Cited in P. E. More and F. L. Cross, *Anglicanism* (London, SPCK, 1935), p.403.

23. *The Works of John Bramhall*, Library of Anglo-Catholic Theology, Vol.X, p.282.

24. Charles Gore *The Church and the Ministry*, third edition (London, Longmans, Green and Co., 1893), p.355. He made a similar claim in *Roman Catholic Claims* (1884), new edition (London, Longmans, Green and Co., 1905), p.65.

25. W. Sanday (ed.), *Different Conceptions of Priesthood and Sacrifice*, (London, Longmans, 1900), p.149.

26. Charles Gore, *Orders and Unity?* (London, John Murray, 1909), pp.83f.

27. *Roman Catholic Claims*, p.141.

28. *The Church and the Ministry*, pp.304, 305.

29. References are to R. C. Moberly, *Ministerial Priesthood* (with an introduction by A. T. Hanson), reprint (London, SPCK, 1969).

30. DS 3315–3319 (13 September 1896). The best survey of the literature is George H. Tavard, *A Review of Anglican Orders: The Problem and the Solution* (Collegeville, Michael Glazier, 1990).

31. On the influence of Moberly, see Terence Card, *Priesthood and Ministry in Crisis* (London, SCM, 1988), as well as A. T. Hanson's introduction to the SPCK reprint (pp. vii–xxi).

32. *The Basis of Anglican Fellowship* (Oxford, Mowbray, 1914), pp.4f.

33. *Catholicism: Roman and Anglican* (London, Hodder and Stoughton, 1899), p.xix.

34. *The Apostolic Ministry* (London, Hodder and Stoughton, 1946), p.52.

35. Cited in David Nicholls, *The Pluralist State* (London and Basingstoke, Macmillan, 1975), p.103.

36. *Contemporary Review* 1899, p.464.

37. *The Present State of Ecclesiastical Architecture in England* (London, 1843), pp.137f.

38. The only biographical account is Maurice G. Tucker, *John Neville Figgis. A Study* (London, SPCK, 1950), Chapter One. Books cited include *Civilisation at the Crossroads* (London, 1912) (thereafter *Civilisation*); *The Divine Right of Kings* (London, 1914); *Churches in the Modern State* (thereafter *CMS*) (London, 1914); *The Fellowship of the Mystery* (thereafter *Fellowship*) (London, 1914). I have looked in more detail at Figgis's ecclesiology in 'Concepts of the Voluntary Church in England and Germany, 1890–1920: A study of J. N. Figgis and Ernst Troeltsch' in *Zeitschrift für neuere Theologiegeschichte*, Vol.2, No.1 (1995), pp.37–59.

39. Fairbairn, *Catholicism: Roman and Anglican*, p.xxi.

40. Cited in H. A. Wilson, *Received with Thanks* (Oxford, Mowbray, 1940), p.118.

41. G. L. Prestige, *The Life of Charles Gore* (London, Heinemann, 1935), p.196.

42. He has, however, recently been influential in political theory. See esp. David Nicholls, *The Pluralist State*; second revised edition, 1994. For a discussion of authority in the Church, see esp. Chapter 7 and Paul Q. Hirst, *Associative Democracy* (Cambridge, Polity Press, 1994), esp. Chapter 2.

43. A. Michael Ramsey, *The Gospel and the Catholic Church* (London, Longmans, Green and Co., 1936), p.66.

44. See, for example, *Gospel and the Catholic Church*, p.84.

45. See, for example, the work of Rowan Williams. A useful programmatic essay is 'What is Catholic Orthodoxy?' in Kenneth Leech and Rowan Williams (eds), *Essays Catholic and Radical* (London, Bowardean, 1983).